CINCO DE MAYO

an Historical Play

by
Mignon L. Bradley

CINCO DE MAYO, AN HISTORICAL PLAY
By Mignon L. Bradley

Published by   LUISA PRODUCTIONS
                        P.O. BOX 6836
                        SANTA BARBARA, CA 93160

                        COPYRIGHT 1981, 1992, 2001
                        BY MIGNON L. BRADLEY
                        SECOND PRINTING 1982
                        THIRD PRINTING 1989
                        FOURTH PRINTING 1990
                        FIFTH PRINTING 1992
                        SIXTH PRINTING 1995
                        SEVENTH PRINTING 1997
                        EIGHTH PRINTING 2001

Permission is granted to the classroom instructor to reproduce materials contained herein for use with his or her students only. Reproduction of any materials contained herein for any other purpose is strictly a violation of United States Copyright Law.

        Printed in U.S.A.

        Library of Congress
        PQ 7079.2B72B72C5 862 81-8341

        ISBN 0-939584-00-X

Table of Contents

Introduction v
Suggestions for Using these Cinco de Mayo Materials 1
    General 1
    Bilingual Cross-Cultural Classes 1
    Primary Grades 1
    Regular Classes 2
    Secondary Level, ESL and Spanish Classes 2
Synopsis (español) 4
Synopsis (English) 5
Los personajes 6
The Characters 7

Cinco de Mayo, una obra histórica 10
Cinco de Mayo, an Historical Play 11
    Prólogo: El plan de la invasión Europea 10
    Prologue: The European Invasion Plan 11
    Acto I: Preparación para la batalla en Puebla 14
    Act I: Preparation for the Battle at Puebla 15
        Escena 1: Los franceses 14
        Scene 1: The French 15
        Escena 2: Los mexicanos 16
        Scene 2: The Mexicans 17
    Acto II: La batalla 22
    Act II: The Battle 23
    Acto III: Maximiliano y Carlota 26
    Act III: Maximilian and Carlota 27
    Acto IV: La ejecución 32
    Act IV: The Execution 33
    Epílogo: Benito Juárez 34
    Epilogue: Benito Juárez 35

Easy-to-Make Costumes and Props 38
Directions for Making Mural Scenery 41

Preview and Review Learning Activities 48
    Vocabulary Activities 48
    Flag Match Game 48
    Geography Games 49
    Character Charades 50
    Poems 51
Cuestionario 52
Pre/Post Quiz 53
Vocabulario/Vocabulary 54

Illustrations and Figures

Flags of Mexico and France 37
Flags of Spain and England 38
Prop and costume details 39
Presidente Benito Juárez 40
General Don Ignácio Zaragoza 40
Napoleon III 40
Maximilian and Carlota 40
French Ship 42
Map of Europe and Mexico 43
Veracruz 44
Puebla 45
Chapultapec Garden 46
Querétero 47

Acknowledgements

My sincere thanks go to the following people for a variety of assistance and encouragement: Jorge Ibañez, Wanda de Paz, Robert Blevitt, Aurora Miller, Dorothy Jacobson Frost, Rose Pueschel, David Duane Frost, Sylvia Ronchietto, Wally Ronchietto, Yolanda Guevarra, David Sanchez, Ana Maria Catalán, Betty Day, and Chico Villegas.

Typography and lay-out by Jim Cook.

Introduction

CINCO DE MAYO (Fifth of May) is a very important holiday celebrated all over Mexico and everywhere people of Mexican heritage reside. The newly independent Mexican Republic, militarily invaded by the French in 1862, rallied together all its supporters, the Mexican Army and the Indians, to defeat the French at Puebla on May, 5, 1862. A typical CINCO DE MAYO FIESTA (party) would include food, colorful dancing and a piñata-breaking for the children.

My concern as an educator is that the reason for all the celebrating be presented, especially for the understanding of those who are not familiar with the holiday. This play was written and has been performed in the interest of better inter-cultural understanding.

The book was especially designed to make performing *Cinco de Mayo* easy, fun and educational for the students, the teacher and the audience. The teacher does not need to spend hours searching for just the right pictures or figuring out how to make scenery and props. While research done by students is beneficial, it is not essential to this production.

In addition to the bilingual script and synopsis, you have in this one easy-to-use volume illustrations and directions for making simple costumes and props, pictures of scenes that can be projected and traced to give large outlines for children to paint as mural scenery, preview and review reinforcement learning activities which include geography, flag and vocabulary games, as well as poems, maps and a pre/post quiz.

Suggestions for Using These Cinco de Mayo Materials

IN GENERAL
1. Discuss Cinco de Mayo with the class using the poems referred to in the Table of Contents and/or contained in the script at the ends of Act II and the Epilogue.
2. Present vocabulary as appropriate using the lists given and the suggested activities.
3. Preview the flags of Mexico, France, Spain and England in games or by having students make flags.
4. Geography can be introduced and reviewed using the suggested geography games.
5. The Quiz can be given initially to provide baseline information. It can be repeated at the close of the unit.
6. Stage directions are always given from the perspective of the performers (i.e., stage-right is the performer's right as s/he faces the audience).
7. Costumes, props and mural scenery can be made for an extended arts and crafts project.

BILINGUAL CROSS-CULTURAL CLASSES
The scripts can be used so that each child performs in her or his stronger language, or in her or his second language, depending upon the focus of the experience.

The synopsis could be read in one language with the play performed in the other language. This could be done act-by-act so the monolinguals in the audience need to remember smaller bits of information at a time.

PRIMARY GRADES
It is especially important that the Narrator be a very good reader, have her or his parts memorized, be a helper from an upper grade, be the teacher, or be a different individual for each act to allow for more polishing.

Individual parts can be memorized even by very young children (Second graders have done it!) if they are given their parts only on slips of paper rather than being handed an entire script, which can be confusing.

REGULAR CLASSES
Most of the script could be done in English with as much Spanish as possible being used on short and simple lines. Even if the teacher does not know Spanish, there may be students in the class who are fully or partially literate in Spanish. This could be an excellent opportunity for that child to assist the teacher and fellow students in learning some Spanish from a Native speaker.

SECONDARY LEVEL
ESL AND SPANISH CLASSES
The scripts could be used for a Reader's Theater performance rather than the more elaborate play production. The poems, the quiz and the vocabulary activities could be used for preview materials; and the games of flags, geography and character charades as well as the quiz serve as valuable follow-up reinforcement activites.

Synopsis

PROLOGO
Con deseos de extender su influencia al Nuevo Mundo, Napoleón Tercero usó las deudas que México tenía con Francia, España e Inglaterra como excusa para invadir militarmente. El plan de la invasión Europea se hace entre oficiales de España, Francia e Inglaterra, incluyendo a Napoleón Tercero.

ACTO I
Los Franceses desembarcan en Veracruz en la **Escena 1**. Su General, Laurences, inmediatamente envía el mensaje a Francia de que no anticipa oposición alguna en su marcha a la capital, México.
En la **Escena 2**, Los Mexicanos se preparan para la batalla. El Presidente Benito Juárez se dedica a la defensa de su patria y pide a su gente unirse en contra de Francia. Los Indios Zacapoaztlas y el General Zaragoza se preparan para la batalla en Puebla.

ACTO II
La batalla consta de tres ataques Franceses, todos sin éxito.

ACTO III
Con mas de treinta mil tropas Francesas,* la intervención sigue. El Archiduque Maximiliano y la Archiduquesa Carlota de Austria fueron nombrados Emperador y Empeatriz de México. Dos Generales del Ejército Imperialista Mexicano de Maximiliano, Miramón y Mejía informan que el poder republicano bajo su líder Benito Juárez sigue creciendo. Napoleón Tercero, bajo la presión de Europa y de los Estados Unidos manda que se retiren todas las tropas Francesas. Carlota viaja a Europa para defender la causa de Maximiliano.

ACTO IV
Maximiliano, Miramón y Mejía son fusilados en Querétaro.

EPILOGO
Discurso de Benito Juárez: "Entre dos individuos como entre naciones, el respeto al derecho ajeno es la paz."

---

*Ni España ni Inglaterra tenía interés en conquistar a México. Los Estados Unidos estaban preocupados con la Guerra Civil, no pudieron intervenir.

Synopsis

PROLOGUE
Desiring to extend his influence to the New World, Napoleon III used the recovery of debts Mexico owed to France, Spain and England as an excuse to invade militarily. The European Invasion Plan is made in the first act among the Spanish, French and English officials, including Napoleon III himself.

ACT I
The French land at Veracuz in **Scene 1** and their General, Laurences, immediately sends word back to France that they anticipate no opposition along their march to the capital, Mexico City.

In **Scene 2**, the Mexican President, Benito Juárez, dedicates himself to the defense of his country and beseeches his people to unite against the French. Zacapoaztlas Indians and General Zaragoza's Army prepare for the battle at Puebla.

ACT II
The battle consists of three French attacks, each one unsuccessful.

ACT III
With thousands of reinforcements from France,* the invasion continues and Maximilian and Carlota, Archduke and Archduchess of Austria, are made Emperor and Empress of Mexico. Two of Maximilian's Imperial Mexican Army Generals, Miramón and Mejía report that republican strength under Benito Juárez's leadership continues to grow. Napoleon III under pressure from Europe and the United States has ordered the withdrawal of all French troops. Carlota leaves for Europe to plead Maximilian's case.

ACT IV
Maximilian, Miramón and Mejía are executed in Querétaro.

EPILOGUE
Benito Juárez's speech: "Between two individuals as between nations, respect for another's rights is Peace!"

---

*Neither Spain nor England was interested in conquering Mexico. The U.S. was preoccupied with the Civil War, unable to intervene.

Los personajes

Prólogo: El plan de la invasión Europea
Narrador
Oficial Inglés
Oficial Español
Oficial Francés
Napoleón Tercero

Acto I: Preparación para la batalla
Escena 1: Los franceses
Narrador
Gen. Laurences
Coronel

Escena 2: Los mexicanos
Narrador
Lucas (Líder de los Indios)
Los Indios Zacapoaztlas
General Zaragoza
Díaz
Berriozabal
Negrete
Benito Juárez
Méndez
Lamadrid
Escobedo
Martínez

Acto II: La batalla
Narrador
El Ejército Mexicano
Los Indios
General Laurences
El Ejército Francés
Lucas

Acto III: Maximiliano y Carlota
Narrador
Maximiliano
Carlota
Gen. Mejía
Gen. Miramón

Acto IV: La ejecución
Narrador
Maximiliano
Mejía
Miramón
Carcelero
Comandante del Escuadrón
Escuadrón de Fusilamiento

Epílogo: Benito Juárez
Benito Juárez
Narrador
Todos

The Characters

Prologue: The European Invasion Plan
Narrator   French Official
English Official   Napoleon III
Spanish Official

Act I: Preparation for the Battle
Scene 1: The French
Narrator   Gen. Laurences   Colonel

Scene 2: The Mexicans
Narrator   Benito Juárez
Lucas (Leader of the Indians)
The Zacapoaztlas Indians
General Zaragoza   Mendez
Díaz   Lamadrid
Berriozabal   Escobedo
Negrete   Martinez

Act II: The Battle
Narrator   General Laurences
The Mexican Army   The French Army
The Indians   Lucas

Act III: Maximilian and Carlota

Narrator   Gen. Mejia
Maximilian   Gen. Miramon
Carlota

Act IV: The Execution
Narrator   Jailer
Maximilian   Firing Squad Commander
Mejía   Firing Squad
Miramón

Epilogue: Benito Juárez
Benito Juárez   Narrator   All

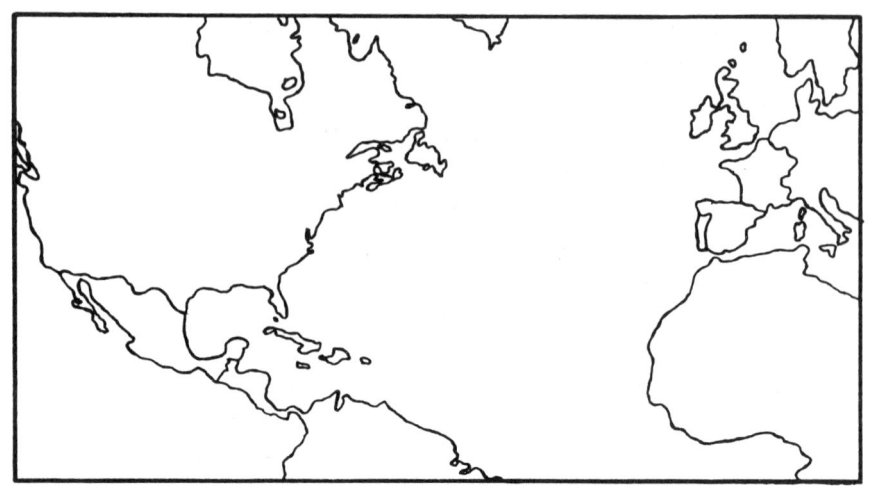

CINCO DE MAYO

an Historical Play

CINCO DE MAYO
Una obra histórica

PROLOGO
EL PLAN DE LA INVASION EUROPEA

ESCENA: Europa con el mapa en la pared.

*(Primero entran **los oficiales, inglés, español y francés**, luego **Napoleón Tercero** cuando los menciona el narrador. Cada uno de los oficiales tiene una bandera de su país que la audiencia puede ver. Mientras habla el narrador, parece que platican ellos pero no hacen ningun ruído en realidad.)*

NARRADOR
En Francia, una junta de oficiales de España, Inglaterra y Francia platican de sus inversiones monetarias hechas al otro lado del Océano Atlántico, en México. Acaban de recibir información del Presidente de México, Benito Juárez de que acausa de condiciones económicas no repagarán los débitos temporálmente *(por algún tiempo)*.

OFICIAL INGLES
¿Qué vamos a hacer cuando México no paga las deudas que tiene con nosotros? Necesitamos el dinero también.

OFICIAL ESPAÑOL
Tenemos que mandar soldados para rescatar nuestro dinero. Nunca deberíamos haberle dado su independencia a México.

OFICIAL FRANCES
El ejército francés es el mejor del mundo y además de rescatar los debitos de México, podemos glorificar el nombre de Napoleón Tercero. Podemos conquistar a México fácilmente.

OFICIAL ESPAÑOL
¡Qué lástima, Benito Juárez! Presidente de México no mas vas a ser.
¡Otra vez la realeza de Europa reinará en El Nuevo Mundo!

CINCO DE MAYO
An Historical Play

PROLOGUE
THE EUROPEAN INVASION PLAN

SCENE: Europe with the map on the wall.

*(First the **English, Spanish** and **French Officials** enter, then **Napoleon III** when each is mentioned by the **Narrator**. Each one of the officials has a flag of his country which is visible to the audience. While the **Narrator** is talking, they mouth words and act as though they are conferencing.)*

NARRATOR
At a conference in France, English, Spanish and French officials including Napoleon III are discussing the financial investments they made across the Atlantic Ocean in Mexico. They have just received word from the president of Mexico, Benito Juárez, that due to serious economic conditions, the debt payments will be suspended temporarily.

ENGLISH OFFICIAL
What are we going to do about Mexico not repaying the debts she owes us? We need the cash too!

SPANISH OFFICIAL
We will have to send troops to recover this money. We should never have given Mexico her independence.

FRENCH OFFICIAL
The French Army is the best in the world and we can not only recover the debts, but we can add glory to the name of Napoleon III. We can easily conquer Mexico!

SPANISH OFFICIAL
Eat your heart out Benito Juárez! President of Mexico you will be no more. Once again European royalty will reign in the New World.

NAPOLEON TERCERO

Mandaré a mi mejor general, Laurences y soldados expertos en barcos a Veracruz inmediatemente. *(Con mirada de locura mueve su mano lentamente como abarcando el horizonte.)* Verán todos que fácilmente sojuzgarán a la gente de México. ¡Agarraremos mucho más que los pequeños debitos prestados a México, agarraremos todo México! *(Frotándose las manos como verdaderos villanos, con miradas diabólicas, salen por la izquierda. Menos el **oficial inglés**, se ríen satanicamente.)*

*(Entre actos, el **oficial frances** entra con un barco en miniatura y lo mueve de Francia a México en el mapa, mientras dice:)*

OFICIAL FRANCES

Y el general francéés, Laurences, y sus hombres viajaron en barco por el Océano Atlántico. *(Dejando el barco, sale.)*

NAPOLEON III

I will send my best general, Laurences, and expert French soldiers in ships to Veracruz immediately. *(Slowly and with a glazed look on his face he gestures with his arm as though he is painting a picture of the future.)* You will all see how easily we will subdue the populations of Mexico. We will take much more than the small debt Mexico owes us; WE WILL TAKE MEXICO!

*(Wringing their hands as true villains, they all have looks of evil glee on their faces as they exit stage-left. Except the **English Official**, they even laugh with devilish delight.)*

*(Between acts, the **French Official** enters stage-left with a miniature ship, which he moves from France to Mexico on the map, as he says:)*

FRENCH OFFICIAL

And the French General Laurences and his men traveled by ship across the Atlantic Ocean to Mexico. *(Leaving the ship attached to the map at Veracruz, he exits stage left.)*

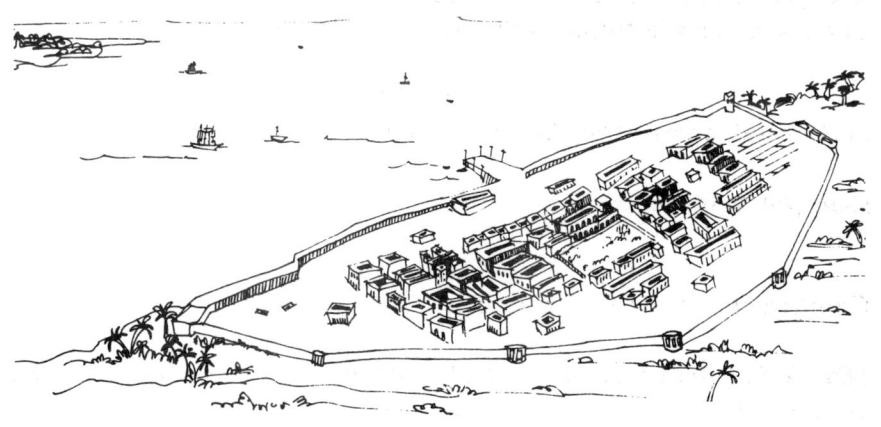

ACTO I
PREPARACION PARA LA BATALLA EN PUEBLA

Escene 1: Los franceses

ESCENA: Veracruz

NARRADOR

El comandante del ejército francés, Laurences llega a Veracruz temprano en marzo de 1862 *(mil ochocientos sesentaidos)*, dos meses antes de la batalla del Cinco de Mayo.

(Laurences y sus hombres entran por la izquierda.)

LAURENCES

Así es Veracruz. ¡Qué campo tan hermoso tiene México! Tengo toda la confianza en que no tendremos ningún problema al sojuzgar al ejército mexicano. ¡Coronel!

CORONEL

Si, General. *(Oui, General)*

GENERAL LAURENCES

Regresa a Francia inmediatamente y diles que el ejército francés ha sojuzgado a la gente de México y ha comenzado su marcha a la capital. Conquistaremos la fortaleza en Puebla sín batalla.

CORONEL

Sí, General, adiós. *(Oui, General, adieu.)*

(Sale por la izquierda.)

LAURENCES

Comenzamos la marcha, hombres.

(En desfile detrás de su general, marchan a la derecha, salen del escenario.)

ACT I:
PREPARATION FOR THE BATTLE AT PUEBLA

SCENE 1: The French

SCENE: Veracruz

NARRATOR
The commander of the French Army, Laurences, arrives in Veracruz in early March 1862, two months before the Cinco de Mayo battle.

*(**Laurences** first, then his men enter from stage left.)*

LAURENCES
So this is Veracruz! What a beautiful country Mexico is. I am quite confident that we will have no problem defeating the Mexican Army. *(In a commanding tone, he says:)* Colonel!

COLONEL
Oui, General. *(Yes, General)*

LAURENCES
Return to France at once and report that the great French Army has subdued the people of Mexico and has begun the march to the capital, Mexico City. The fort at Puebla will be taken easily, probably without even a battle.

COLONEL
Oui, General, adieu! *(Yes, General, good-bye!)*

*(The **Colonel** exits stage-left.)*

LAURENCES
(In a commanding tone to his soldiers) Let us begin the march, men!

(In formation behind their commander Laurences, the soldiers march off stage-right.)

Escena 2: Los mexicanos

ESCENA: Puebla.

NARRADOR
Benito Juárez oyó que los franceses planeaban un ataque y se dedica a defender a su país.

(Entra por la derecha Benito Juárez y un gentío mirándolo inmediatamente, de espaldas hacia la audiencia.)

BENITO JUAREZ
Somos un pueblo. Tenemos que unificarnos y olvidar cualquier diferencia que tuviéramos y proteger nuestro México amado contra los invasores extranjeros. Cada uno de nosotros es importante. Preparémonos.

¡Viva la República de México!

GENTIO
¡Viva la República de México!

(Juárez sale del escenario por la derecha.)

NARRADOR
En las montañas de Puebla, los Zacapoaztlas se juntaron para eschuchar a su líder Lucas.

(Entra Lucas llevando sarape y huaraches, indios vestidos de la misma manera, también indias llevando rebozos y con sus hijos. Los indios, todos se sientan mirando a Lucas inmediatemente cuando entra.)

LUCAS
Nuestro hermano Benito Juárez y nuestra patria amada necesitan nuestra ayuda ahora. Los soldados franceses marchan de Veracruz y tenemos que detenerlos. Preparémonos para la batalla que se llevará a cabo en la fortaleza de Puebla.

TODOS LOS INDIOS
¡Los franceses no se adueñarán de nuestra tierra!

SCENE 2: The Mexicans

SCENE: Puebla.

NARRATOR
Benito Juárez heard that the French planned an attack and dedicated himself to the defense of his country.

*(Enter right, **Benito Juárez** and a **crowd** of people who immediately sit on the floor facing him, their backs to the audience.)*

BENITO JUAREZ
We are all one people. We must unite and forget any differences we may have had and protect our beloved Mexico from these foreign invaders. Each one of us is important. Let us prepare! Long live the Republic of Mexico!

CROWD
Long live the Republic of Mexico!

*(**Benito Juárez** exits stage-right.)*

NARRATOR
In the mountains of Puebla, the Zacapoaztlas Indians gather to listen to their leader, Lucas.

*(Enter **Lucas** wearing sarape and huaraches and **Indian men** dressed similarly; also **Indian women**, wearing rebozos, with their **children**. Indians sit facing Lucas immediately upon entering just as did Juárez's audience.)*

LUCAS
Our brother Benito Juárez and our beloved country need our help now. French soldiers are marching from Veracruz and we must stop them. We must prepare ourselves for a battle that will soon take place at the Fort at Puebla.

ALL INDIANS
The French will not take our land! *(said in unison, with conviction)*

(Todos los indios incluyendo a Lucas salen del escenario.)

NARRADOR

El General Don Ignácio Zaragoza era el comandante *(jefe)* del ejército mexicano. *(Entra **Zaragosa** y entran los demás cuando los menciona el narrador),* Berriozabal, Negrete, Díaz, Mendez, Lamadrid, Escobedo y Martinez, todos se harán héroes famosos en la historia mexicana a causa del valor y coraje que mostraron el cinco de mayo de mil ochocientos sesentaidós (1862) en Puebla. *(Ponen mucha atención a lo que dice el Gen. Zaragoza.)*

ZARAGOZA
Martínez, tu y tus hombres vayan a la torre norte.

MARTINEZ
Sí, comandante.

ZARAGOZA
Mendez, tú y tus hombres formen a lo largo de la muralla *(el muro)* del este.

MENDEZ
Sí, comandante

ZARAGOZA
Negrete, tú y tus hombres mantengan el establo.

NEGRETE
¡Como nunca, jefe!

ZARAGOZA
Berriozabal, a la muralla del norte. Lamadrid, a la muralla del sur.

BERRIOZABAL
Sí, comandante.

LAMADRID
Sí, comandante.

(Indians including Lucas exit left.)

NARRATOR
General Don Ignácio Zaragoza was the commander of the Mexican forces. *(Zaragoza enters and the others enter as the narrator mentions them)*, Berriozabal, Negrete, Díaz, Mendez, Lamadrid, Escobedo, and Martinez were all to become famous heroes in Mexican history as a result of the valor and courage they displayed on May 5, 1862, in Puebla.

*(These **military men** gather into a semi-circle so that all are visible to the audience and they listen for their orders from **Zaragoza**.)*

ZARAGOZA
Martinez, you and your men take the north tower.

MARTINEZ
Si, comandante. *(Yes, commander.)*

ZARAGOZA
Mendez, you and your men position yourselves along the east wall.

MENDEZ
Si, comandante.

ZARAGOZA
Negrete, you and your men defend the stables.

NEGRETE
Like they've never before been defended! Yes, sir!

ZARAGOZA
Berriozabal, take the north rampart *(wall)*, Lamadrid, the south wall.

BERRIOZABAL
Si, comandante!

LAMADRID
Si, comandante!

ZARAGOZA
Escobedo, tú y tus hombres asegúrense que los franceses no entrarán por el oeste.

ESCOBEDO
Sí, comandante, está hecho.

ZARAGOZA
Díaz, tu grupo es más grande. Asegúrate que tus hombres se dispersen y vayan a los lugares de ofensiva francesa mas fuerte.

DIAZ
Si, comandante. ¡Derrotaremos a los franceses hoy!

TODOS
¡Derrotaremos a los franceses hoy!

ZARAGOZA
¡Viva la República, la Libertad y la Reforma!

TODOS
¡Viva la República, la Libertad y la Reforma!

(Todos salen por la izquierda.)

ZARAGOZA
Escobedo, you and your men make sure that the French do not come in from the west.

ESCOBEDO
Si, comandante. Está hecho. *(yes, sir. It's done!)*

ZARAGOZA
Díaz, your group is largest. See that your men disperse themselves to the positions of heaviest French offensives.

DIAZ
Si, comandante. We will defeat the French today!

ALL
We will defeat the French today!

ZARAGOZA
Long live the Republic, Liberty and Reform!

ALL
Long live the Republic, Liberty and Reform!!

(They all exit left.)

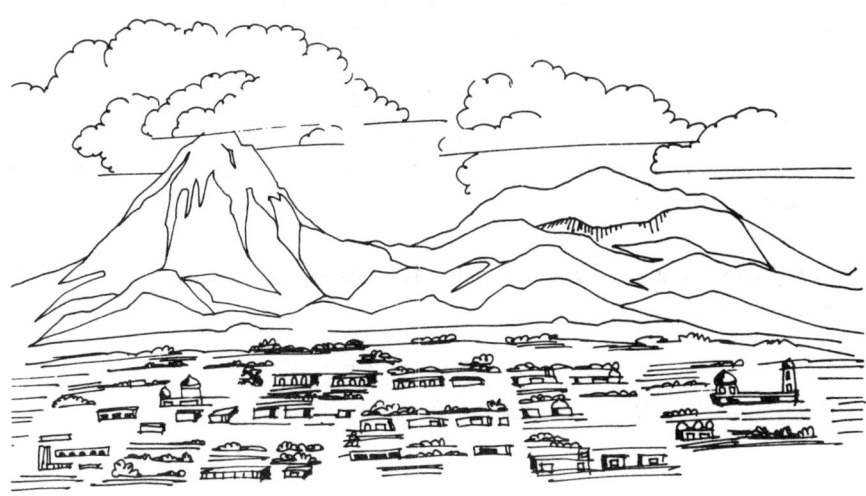

ACTO II
LA BATALLA

ESCENA: Puebla

(El ejército mexicano entra por la izquierda llevando un fuerte hecho de papel en frente de ellos. Se mueven hacia el centro de la escena y paran. Laurences y el ejército frances entran lentamente por la derecha. Laurences les indica con su brazo que se adelanten hasta pocos pies del fuerte. Todos en el escenario dejan de moverse, Laurences sube su brazo y luego grita mientras lo baja.)

LAURENCES
¡Disparen!

(Todos hacen sonidos de disparos. La batalla es de movimiento lento y dura no más que treinta segundos. Los franceses avanzan lentamente hacia el ejército mexicano. Algunos franceses caen. Los franceses se retiran, salen del escenario caminando por la derecha, arrastrando a sus heridos.)

LUCAS
¡Matémos a los franceses!

NARRADOR
Los franceses estaban muy sorprendidos de que los mexicanos hicieran tan gran defensa. Se retiraron para reunirse y atacar otra vez.

LAURENCES
(En el escenario a la derecha hablando a sus hombres.) ¡Increíble! No los derrotamos en el primer ataque. Tenemos que enfrentarlos con más cuidado. ¿Listos?

(Los frances responden afirmativamente con sus cabezas mientras entran lentamente.)

LAURENCES
(Subiendo su rifle y gritando otra vez.) ¡Disparen!

ACT II
THE BATTLE

SCENE: Puebla countryside. A fort is brought in by the Mexican Army.

*(The **Mexican Army** enters from the left holding a paper fort in front of them. They move almost to center stage and stop. **Laurences** enters slowly from the right. He motions to his men with a sweeping arm indicating that they come forward. The **French Army** enters to center-stage a few feet short of the fort. **Everyone** on stage stops moving. **Laurences** holds up his arm and then shouts as he lowers it:)*

LAURENCES
Fire!

*(**Soldiers** make shooting sound effects. The **French** advance slowly on the **Mexican Army**. Combat is in SLOW MOTION and lasts about 30 seconds. Some **French Soldiers** fall to the ground. The **French** retreat, exit backwards to stage-right, dragging their injured off with them.)*

LUCAS
¡Matémos a los Franceses! *(Let us destroy the French!)*

NARRATOR
The French were very surprised that the Mexicans put up so much resistance. They retreated to regroup their forces and present another attack.

LAURENCES
(Just on-stage, talking to his forces just off-stage.) Incredible! We didn't destroy them on the first attack. We must take more care to aim carefully. Ready men?

*(**French** are nodding affirmatively as they enter stage slowly.)*

LAURENCES
(Holding up his rifle, he shouts:) Fire!

(Los frances avanzan un poco. Todos hacen sonidos de disparos por unos quince segundos. Más soldados franceses caen y Laurences grita.)

LAURENCES
¡Alto el fuego!

(Otra vez los franceses serítaran arrastrando a sus compatriotas heridos.)

NARRADOR
No tuvieron éxito en adueñarse del fuerte de Puebla, otra vez. Trataron los franceses una vez más.

(Entran los franceses.)

LAURENCES
(Subiendo y bajando su brazo con el rifle mientras dice:) ¡Ataquen!

(Todos hacen sonidos de disparos. Caen la mitad de soldados franceses.)

LAURENCES
¡Retírense!

(Los franceses salen arrastrando sus heridos.)

NARRADOR
Tres ataques en todo ese cinco de mayo, pero el ejército mexicano mostró su superioridad.

LUCAS
¡Qué salgan los franceses de México y nunca regresen!

TODO EL EJERCITO MEXICANO
¡Alto el fuego! regimientos y escuadrones!
Ya no tiren, ya corrieron los frentones,
¡Toquen diana, clarines y tambores!
¡Gloria al Cinco de Mayo que triunfó!

(Gritan con los brazos en alto, luego salen del escenario por la izquierda.)

*(The **French forces** advance a little. **All** make shooting sounds for about 15 seconds. A few more **French soldiers** fall. Laurences shouts:)*

LAURENCES
Cease fire!

*(Again the **French** back off-stage dragging their fallen.)*

NARRATOR
Again the French forces were unable to take the fort at Puebla. They made one more attempt.

*(**French Army** enters.)*

LAURENCES
(Raising his arm with rifle and lowering it as he says) Attack!

*(All soldiers make shooting sounds. Half the **French Soldiers** fall.)*

LAURENCES
Retreat!

*(**French** exit dragging off injured.)*

NARRATOR
Three attacks in all that Cinco de Mayo, but the Mexican Army proved their superiority.

LUCAS
May the French leave Mexico and never return!

ALL MEXICAN ARMY
Hold fire! regiments and squadrons.
They no longer shoot, the enemy has fled.
Sound the bugles, beat the drums.
Hail the victorious Fifth of May!

(They cheer with their right arms up and then exit stage-left.)

ACTO III
MAXIMILIANO Y CARLOTA

ESCENA: El jardín del castillo de Chapultapec.

NARRADOR

Con más de treinta mil tropas franceses, la intervención seguía. Maximiliano Archduque de Austria y su esposa Carlota de Bélgica se hicieron Emperador y Empeatriz de México viviendo en el Castillo de Chapultapec.

(Entran Maximiliano y Carlota por la derecha.)

MAXIMILIANO

La gran família Hapsburgo de Austria respondió al mandado de la gente de México. Aquí estamos en México, Carlota.

CARLOTA

Si, México es un país muy hermoso, pero parece que hay muchos problems. Benito Juárez en el norte y los conservadores aquí en la capital amenazan nuestro poder.

(Entran el General Mejía y el General Miramón del ejército imperial , el ejército de Maximiliano. Maximiliano por la derecha.)

GENERAL MEJIA

(Haciendo reverencia a Carlota:) Buenos días, su majestad. *(Haciendo una reverencia a Maximiliano:)* Buenos días, su majestad.

MAXIMILIANO Y CARLOTA

(Moviendo las cabezas ligeramente.) Buenos días.

GENERAL MIRAMON

(Haciendo una reverencia) Buenos días, su majestad *(otra reverencia).* Buenos días, su majestad.

MAXIMILIANO Y CARLOTA

(Movienda las cabezas ligeramente) Buenos días.

MAXIMILIANO

¿Qué tal?

ACT III:
MAXIMILIAN AND CARLOTA

SCENE: In the garden of Chapultapec Castle.

NARRATOR
With more than 30,000 French soldiers, the Intervention continued. Maximilian, Archduke of Austria, and his wife Carlota of Belgium became the Emperor and Empress of Mexico residing at Chapultapec Castle. *(Enter **Maximilian** and **Carlota** from stage-right.)*

MAXIMILIAN
The great Hapsburg family of Austria has responded to the mandate of the Mexican people. Here we are in Mexico, Carlota.

CARLOTA
Yes, Mexico certainly is a beautiful country, but there seems to be no end to the problems. Benito Juárez in the north and the conservatives here in Mexico City threaten our power.

*(Enter **Mejía** and **Miramón** of the Mexican Imperial Army, Maximilian's Army, from stage-left.)*

GENERAL MEJIA
(Bowing gracefully to the waist, first to Carlota:) Good-day, your majesty. *(Then bowing to Maximilian:)* Good-day, your majesty.

MAXIMILIAN & CARLOTA
(Nod heads slightly and return the greeting:) Good-day.

GENERAL MIRAMON
(Bowing to the waist first to Carlota, then to Maximilian) Good-day, your majesty. Good-day, your majesty.

MAXIMILIAN & CARLOTA
(Nod heads slightly and return the greeting:) Good-day.

MAXIMILIAN
What's up?

GENERAL MEJIA
Tenemos noticias de los Estados Unidos y más noticias acerca de Benito Juárez y los republicanos.

GENERAL MIRAMON
Benito Juárez y su grupo de indios y otros compatriotas tienen control de todas las regiones del norte. El poder republicano crece.

MAXIMILIANO
Presentía eso. Tenemos que capturar y castigar a todos los republicanos, a todos los compatriotas de Juárez. Ojalá que pudiéramos capturar a Juárez.

GENERAL MEJIA
Ya hemos castigado a muchos partidarios de Juárez. Desafortunadamente, los Estados Unidos han mandado que todos los poderes de Europa salgan de la América del Norte inmediatemente. Esta orden sigue La Doctrina de Monroe.

MAXIMILIANO
Recibí información de que Napoleón Tercero mandará que regresen a Francia sus tropas.

CARLOTA
Regresaré ahorita a Francia para pedir a Napoleón que no retire sus tropas. Seguro que me escuchará a mí, la hija de Leopoldo de Bélgica. Adiós, mi amor.

MAXIMILIANO
Date prisa, querida mía. *(La besa.)* Me quedo aquí para defender nuestro trono.

(Carlota sale del escenario por la derecha.)

GENERAL MEJIA
Mantendremos control de México sin la ayuda de Napoleón.

GENERAL MIRAMON
No será fácil.

GENERAL MEJIA
We have news from the United States, and more news about Benito Juárez and his Republicans.

GENERAL MIRAMON
Benito Juárez and his group of Indians and other compatriots have control now in all regions of the north. Republican strength is mounting (increasing).

MAXIMILIAN
I was afraid of that. We must continue to capture and punish all Republicans, all followers of Juárez. If only we could capture Juárez himself.

GENERAL MEJIA
Unfortunately, the United States supports Juárez and has demanded that all European powers leave North America. They call this policy the Monroe Doctrine.

MAXIMILIAN
I received word that Napoleon will order the return of his Army.

CARLOTA
I will return to France at once and ask Napoleon not to withdraw his soldiers. Surely he will listen to me, daughter of Belgium's Leopold I. Good-bye darling.

MAXIMILIAN
Please be quick, my love. *(He kisses her.)* I will stay and defend our throne.

(Carlota exits right.)

GENERAL MEJIA
We will maintain control of Mexico even without Napoleon's help.

GENERAL MIRAMON
It won't be easy.

(Mejía y Miramón salen del escenario por la izquierda.)

MAXIMILIANO

Tengo que preservar el honor, el honor de la familia Hapsburgo. *(Con una mirada preocupada en la cara sale a la derecha.)*

(Mejía and Miramón exit left.)

MAXIMILIAN
I must preserve honor, the Hapsburg honor. *(With a worried look on his face, he exits right.)*

ACTO IV
LA EJECUCION

ESCENA: Querétaro

NARRADOR
A pesar de la súplicas de Carlota a Napoleón en Paris y a El Papa Pío IX en Roma, todos los soldados franceses se retiraron de México. Juárez y los republicanos reconquistaron la capital forzando a Maximiliano a que se rindiera o abandonara la capital. Maximiliano y su ejército salieron a Querétaro donde fueron rodeados y capturados. Para mostrar al mundo que nunca habría un imperio extranjero en México y que todos son iguales según las leyes de México, Maximiliano y los dos generales principales fueron juzgados y fusilados. La ejecución se llevó acabo el 19 de junio de 1867, en Querétaro.

*(Entran el carcelero, **Mejía, Miramón** y **Maximiliano** por la derecha. El **escuadrón de fusilamiento** y su **comandante** entran por la izquierda.)*

COMANDANTE DEL ESCUADRON
¡Listos...Apunten...Fuego!

*(Caen **Maximiliano** y **los generales**. **Los soldados** salen por la izquierda marchando. Regresan sin rifles y arrastran a **Miramón, Mejía** y **Maximiliano** por la izquierda.)*

ACT IV
THE EXECUTION

SCENE: Querétaro.

NARRATOR

Despite Carlota's pleas to Napoleon III in Paris, and to Pope Pius IX in Rome, all French troops were withdrawn from Mexico. Juárez and his Republicans reconquered Mexico City forcing Maximilian to surrender or flee the city. Maximilian and his tiny army fled to Querétaro, where they were surrounded and captured. To show the world that there would be no foreign empires in Mexico and to show that all were equal under Mexican law, Maximilian and his two leading generals, Mejía and Miramón, were court-martialed and sentenced to death by firing squad. The execution took place on June 19, 1867, in Querétaro.

(Led by a jailer, Mejía, Miramón and Maximilian enter from stage-right. The Firing Squad, led by the Squad Sargeant enter marhcing from stage-left.)

SQUAD SARGEANT
Ready... Aim... Fire!

(Maximilian and the Generals fall. The Squad marches out in formation just as they entered from stage-left. They return without their rifles and drag Miramón, Mejía and Maximillan off stage-left.)

EPILOGO
BENITO JUAREZ

ESCENA: Mapa grande o bandera grande de México.

*(Entra **Benito Juárez** y de una manera muy poderosa y llena de dignidad dice en sus propias palabras.)*

BENITO JUAREZ
"Entre dos individuos como entre naciones, el respeto al derecho ajeno es la paz."

NARRADOR
Con la República Mexicana restaurada, canciones y poemas orgullosos y triunfantes emergían de la gente:

>¡Viva Juárez, mexicanos!
>¡Qué viva la Libertad!
>Ya todos somos hermanos,
>¡Qué viva la capital!
>¡Qué vivan todos los libres,
>vivan los bravos soldados!
>¡Qué vivan y qué revivan,
>toditos los mexicanos!

EPILOGUE
BENITO JUAREZ

SCENE: Large map or flag of Mexico.

(Benito Juárez enters and in a most powerful and dignified manner says his own famous quote)

BENITO JUAREZ
"Between two individuals as between nations, respect for another's rights is Peace!"

NARRATOR
With the Mexican Republic restored, proud and triumphant songs and poems emerged from the people:

> Long live Juárez, Mexicans!
> Long live Liberty!
> We are all brothers and sisters!
> Long live the Capital!
> Long live the free!
> Long live the brave soldiers!
> May all Mexicans
> Live brave and free forever!

Presidente Benito Juárez

| GREEN | WHITE | RED |

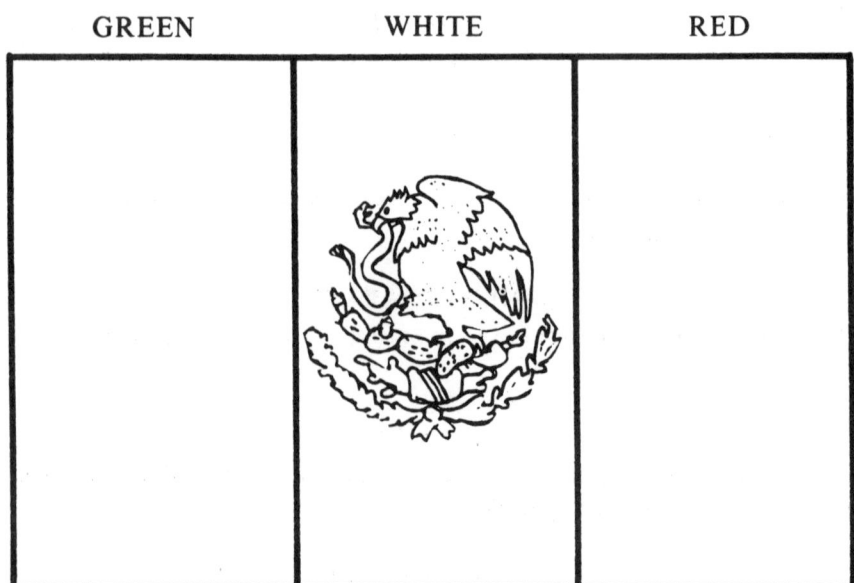

Flag of Mexico/México—Color the eagle brown, the serpent green, the rock brown, the cactus and wreath green, and the bow red.

| RED | WHITE | BLUE |

Flag of France/Francia

Flag of England/Inglaterra—The large red cross is red, framed in white. The diagonal lines are red in the center, surrounded by white, with blue triangles.

Flag of Spain/España—Yellow in center, red above and below.

Easy-to-Make Costumes and Props

1. THE FORT can be made from 48"×36" brown construction paper. Along the side designated as the "top" of the fort wall, cut out six-inch squares every six inches. Use black marking pen, crayon or tempera paint to draw brick construction lines.

2. SOLDIERS HATS, green for Mexican soldiers and blue for French soldiers, can be made by stapling the four-inch ends of 18"×4" construction paper to fit each child's head. A FLAG representing the soldier's country may be reproduced and colored appropriately by the child, then attached to the front of the hat.

3. MACHETE, 4. SWORD, 5. BAYONET can be projected to desired size, using an opaque projector. Trace in pencil and cut out of very stiff cardboard. Cover the cardboard with aluminum foil on the blade and black tape for the handle. The Zacapoaztlas would have the machetes, the regular army soldiers would have either sword or rifle, or rifle with bayonet.

6. RIFLE can be made from two sheets of 12"×18" brown construction paper. To make the barrel, roll the paper lengthwise and tape it. To make the stock, fold the paper on the dotted lines as indicated in drawings (6a) and (6b). Attach the barrel to the stock with tape. Bayonet may be attached to the barrel of the rifles of the French soldiers.

COSTUMES should approximate the styles of those shown in the drawings. The French soldiers wore blue. The Mexicans could be less uniformly dressed since many were Indians dressed in huaraches and sarapes. In the *Prologue*, the French, Spanish and English officials can hold 12"×18" construction-paper flags as identifiers of the nation they each represent.

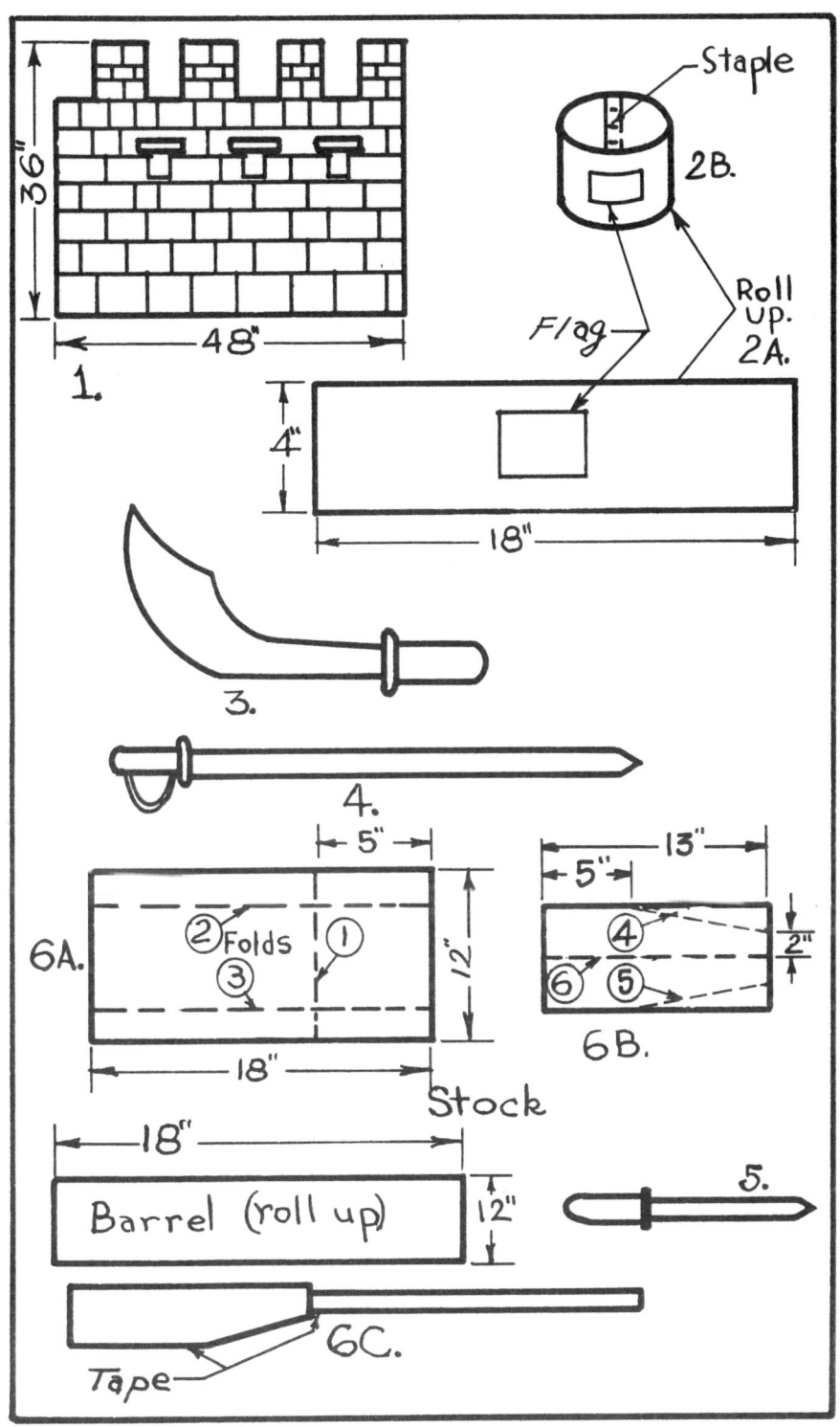

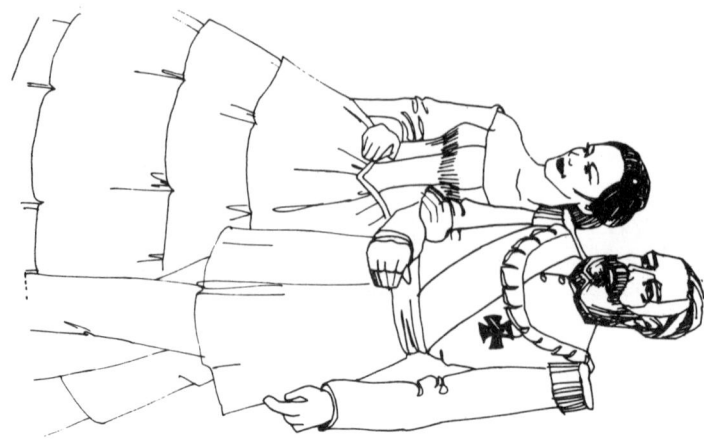

Maximilian and Carlota

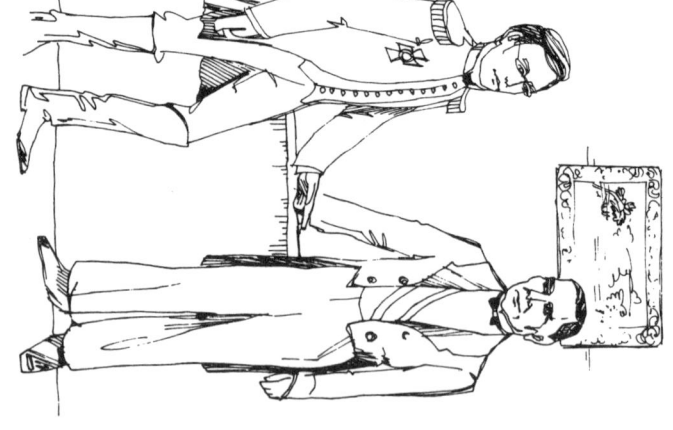

Presidente Benito Juárez and General Don Ignácio Zaragoza

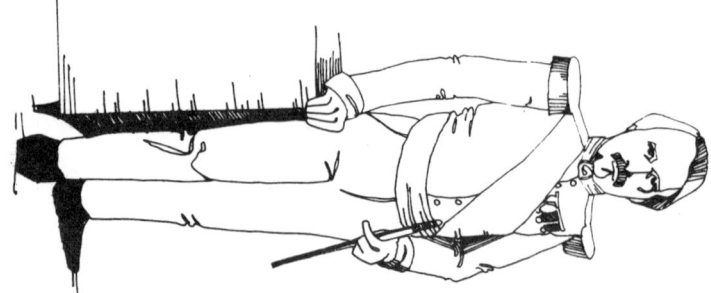

Napoleon III

Directions for Making Mural Scenery

Materials needed:

1. Opaque projector
2. Extension cord
3. Bulletin-board paper (white or desired color)*
4. Masking tape
5. Pencil
6. Brushes
7. Tempera paints
8. Containers for mixing paints

1. Tape paper the size you want your backdrop to be to a wall or chalkboard.

2. Using an opaque projector, project the scene on the paper adjusting it to the desired size. (It is important to use an extension cord long enough to permit movement the length of the room, especially if a very large projection is desired.)

3. Trace the lines carefully with a pencil.

4. Place traced scene on the floor with newspapers surrounding the edges for easy tempera painting and clean-up.

5. Mix desired colors and paint with slightly diluted tempera paint.

*Blue bulletin-board paper gives a fullness to the mural even when the students do not paint every inch of it.

SCENERY BY ACT WITH COLOR SUGGESTIONS

Prologue   Map of European nations, the Atlantic Ocean and Mexico. Paint countries light brown and ocean light blue. Let dry. Add a few darker blue waves. Do outline and lettering in black.

Between Acts	French ship guided from France to Mexico. On white construction paper, outline ship in black; hull and masts are brown.
Act I Scene 1	Veracruz. First paint soil sandy brown and water blue-green. Let dry. Paint vegetation green with brown tree trunks. Buildings are white and brown, with some red tile roofs. Ships have white sails and brown hulls.
Scene 2	Puebla. The famous volcanoes Popocatepetl and Ixtacihuatl have snow caps and are purplish. Closer mountains are blue then brown. Buildings and vegetation as in Veracruz.
Act II	Same Puebla landscape, but with a paper fort brought in by the Mexican soldiers. Directions for fort in *Easy-to-Make Props*.
Act III	Garden of Chapultapec Castle.
Act IV	Querétero. Earth tones, aqueduct is white.
Epilogue	Large map or flag of Mexico; map colors in prologue, flag colors on Flags page.

French Ship

Map of Europe and Mexico

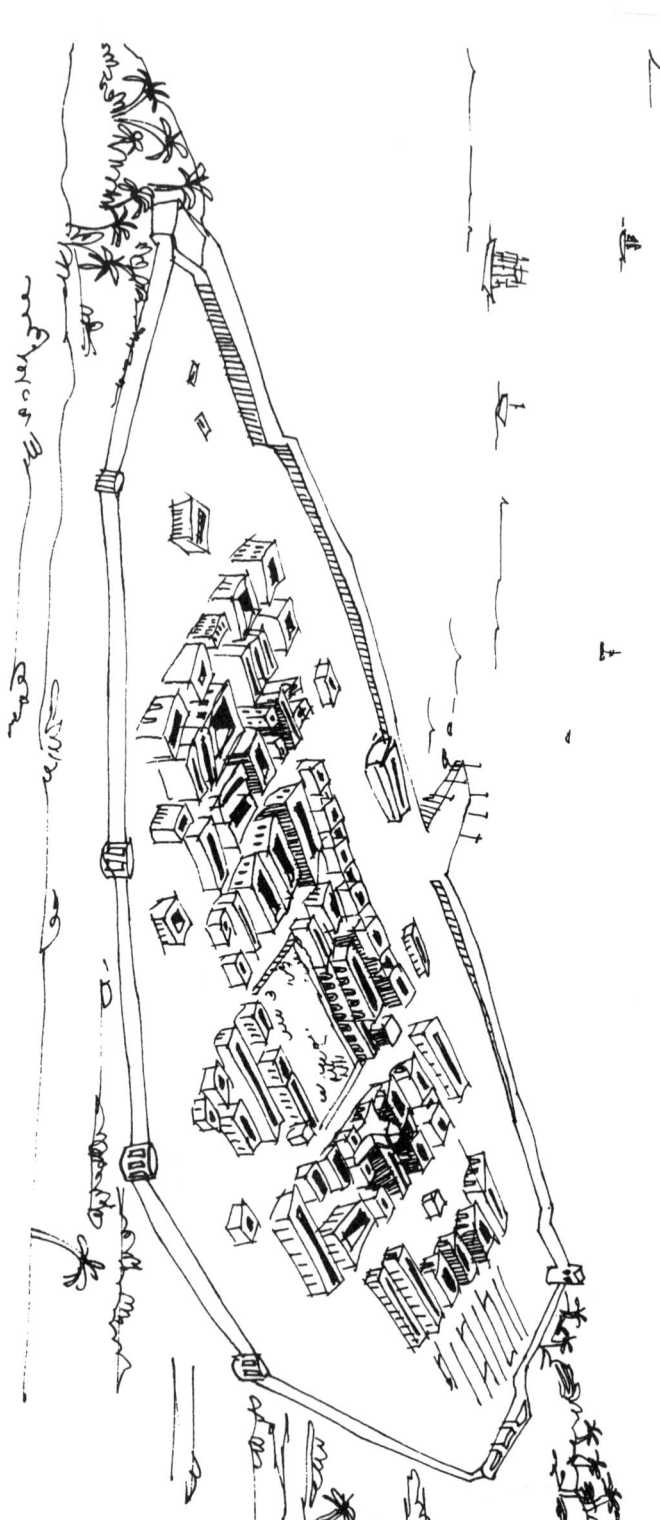

Veracruz

Puebla

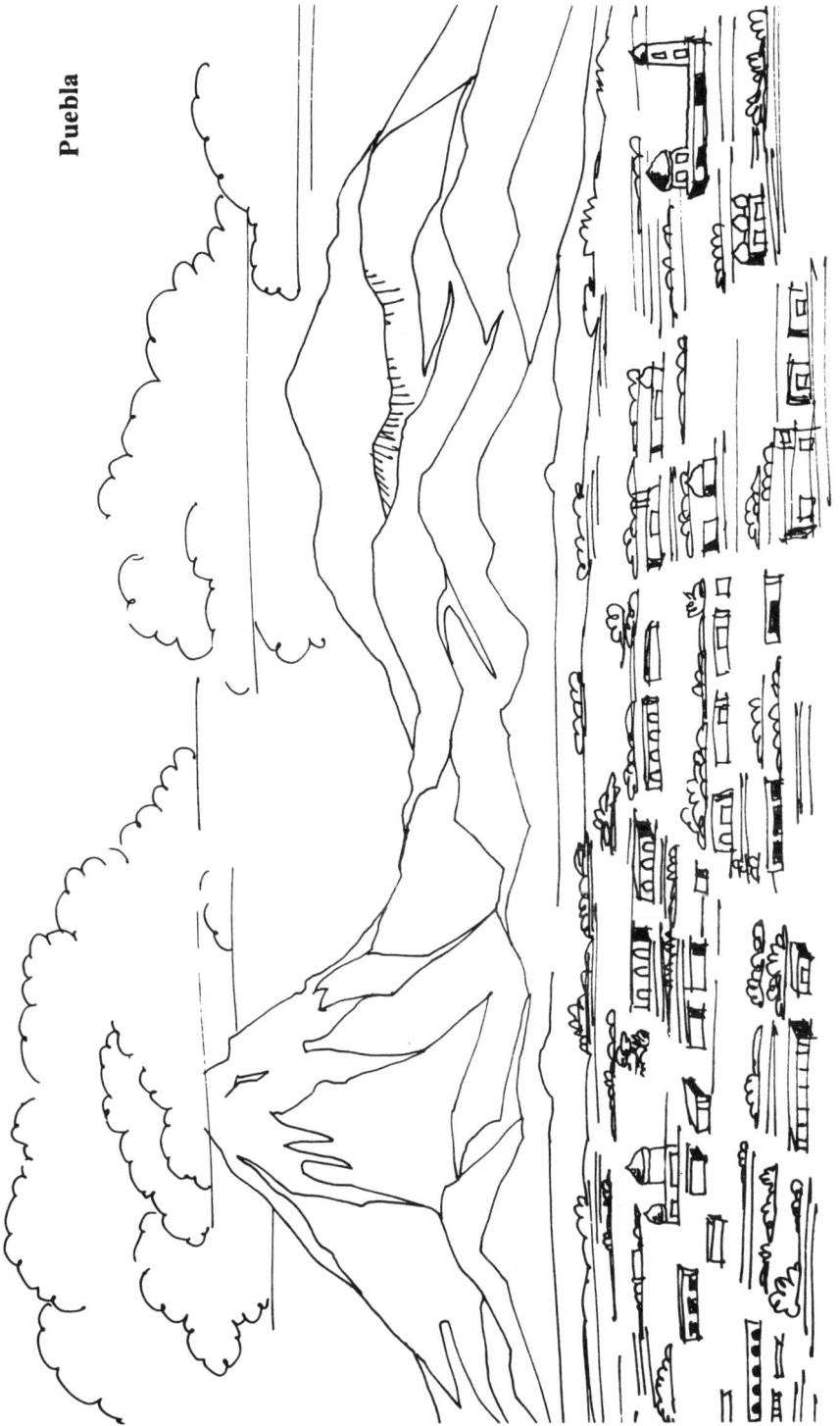

Chapultapec Garden

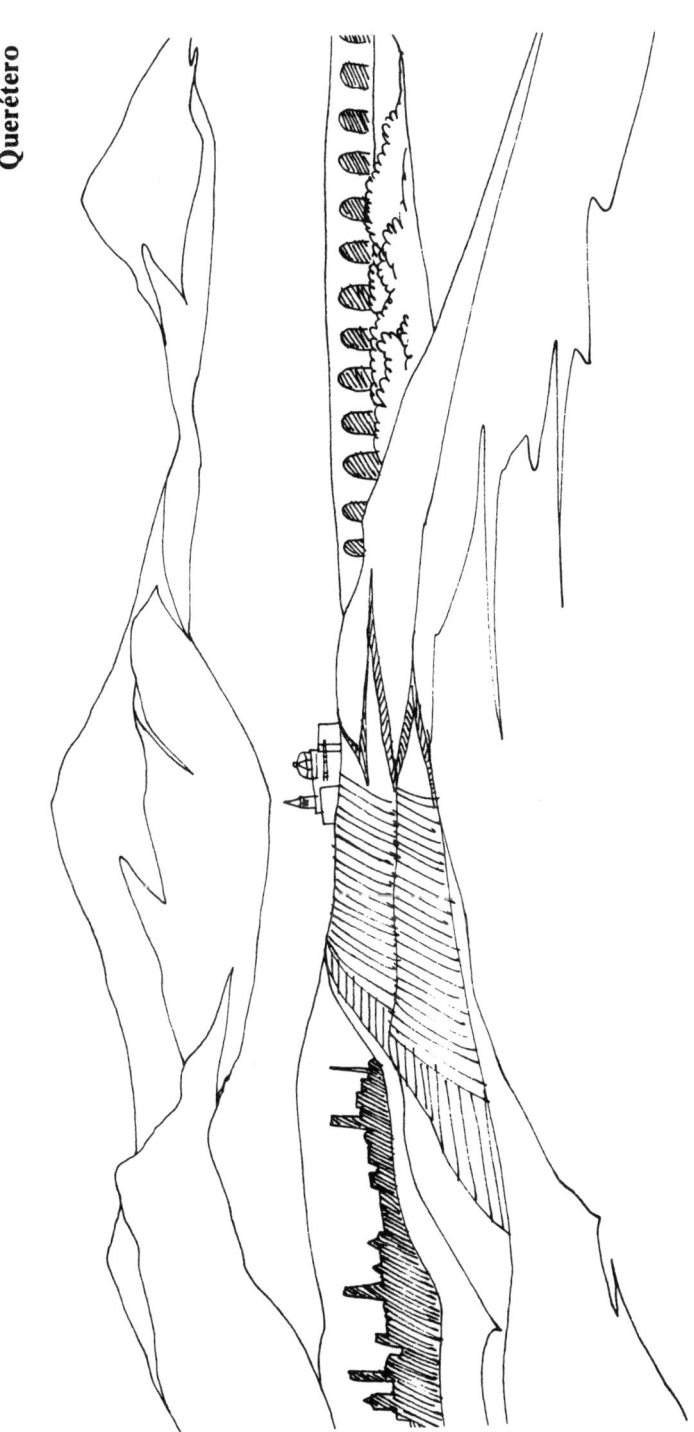

Querétero

Preview and Review Learning Activities

VOCABULARY ACTIVITIES

VOCABULARY INTRODUCTION
Print selected words on cards and tape them to the chalkboard. Ask students to volunteer to read a word they know and to tell about it. When done, the student may take the card. When all words have been discussed, cards may be exchanged by one at a time standing and requesting another volunteer to use the word in a sentence.

VOCABULARY CONCENTRATION (MATCH)
Have students print selected words on cards and print corresponding definitions on other cards (all alike). To play, turn all cards face down. Turn cards up two at a time attempting to match the words with its definition. If a match is not made, the cards are turned back down and it is another's turn. If a match is made, those cards are taken from the arrangement and count as points for the one who matched them. The child who matches the most words with their definitions is the winner.

VOCABULARY "20 QUESTIONS"
One person thinks of a word and others have 20 questions to guess it.

HANGMAN
Hangman may also be played to review vocabulary.

FLAG MATCH GAME

PREPARATION
Reproduce flags of Mexico, France, Spain and England on opaque paper. Students can add color to flags with paint, crayon, or by gluing on construction paper of the appropriate colors. On the same size papers, print the names of the nations in one language per paper.

TO PLAY
The four flags and eight nation names (four in English and four in Spanish) are turned down in an ordered arrangement. Students take turns turning up two papers at a time, attempting to match the flag with the name of the country in Spanish and in English.

GEOGRAPHY GAMES

GEOGRAPHY MATCH
Same as FLAG MATCH except with unnamed outline maps of countries reproduced on papers the same size as the flags.

MASTER GEOGRAPHER
Have two students at a time go to a very large world map displayed for the entire class to see. With their arms at their sides, they listen for the name of a continent, country or body of water. (On a sufficiently detailed map of Mexico, for example, names of cities could be used.)

Once you call out one of the locations listed, the students attempt to point at it. The first to locate and point to the place on the map wins that competition. Those two are seated and another two do the same. Keep a record of the the winners.

This may be repeated to reinforce learning, and other places may be used to continue the game through a round-robin-type elimination process. Once everyone has played once, half are winners. The winners play winners until only half of them have won twice. Those who have won twice play one another and so forth until only one remains, the Master Geographer.

TEAM GEOGRAPHY
Divide children into two teams and give each child a number which corresponds to a child of similar geographic skill on the opposite team. The teams, names and numbers should be written and easily visible. Call out a number, wait for one child from each team to go to the map, then call out a location for them to find. A point for their team goes to the child who locates the place first by pointing to it on the map. The winning team has the most points.

Points to Locate:

Europe	Atlantic Ocean	Belgium
North America	Veracruz	Italy
England	Puebla	Rome
Spain	Mexico City	Austria
France	Querétaro	Paris
Mexico	Northern Mexico	United States

CHARACTER CHARADES

1. Print the names of all the characters on slips of paper (lists of characters preceed each script).
2. Fold the papers and place them in a box or hat.
3. Select a student to draw a character which s/he will silently imitate for the class.
4. Other students attempt to guess which character is being portrayed by raising hands to name the character.
5. The child who correctly guesses the character being portrayed has earned the next opportunity to select another slip of paper and imitate the character named on it.

TEAM CHARACTER CHARADES
Divide students into two teams and keep a record of the number of seconds each team needs to guess character portrayals. The team with the fewest total seconds is the winner.

General Don Ignácio Zaragoza

Poems

You may wish to begin your introductory lesson on CINCO DE MAYO with a discussion of "What is Cinco de Mayo?" and these poems:

The Fifth of May for México

The Fifth of May
No matter what some say,
Is not the Mexican Independence Day.

In eighteen sixty-two,
The French who sailed the ocean blue,
At Puebla met their Waterloo.

To conquer all was why they came.
Amazed by what they saw that day,
Proud and strong the fort did stay.
They'd lost the game they came to play.

For Mexico, the Fifth of May's
A day of pride to glorify.
They trounced the French, they beat the foe,
And celebrate with lots of show.

Zaragoza y Negrete

¡Viva Puebla de Zaragoza y la espada de Negrete!
venció a la Francia orgullosa porque es general valiente...
¡Viva el cumpleaños dichoso que la escuadra francesa perdió,
Zaragoza y Negrete triunfó en el Cinco de Mayo gloriosa...

For more poems, see pages 24, 25, 34 and 35.

Cuestionario Sobre el Cinco de Mayo
(A Ser Realizado Antes Y Después de La Obra)

1. Napoleón Tercero sostuvo que mandaba tropas a México para rescatar deudas que tiene con: (a) Francia, España e Inglaterra, (b) Rusia, Alemania e Italia, o (c) Suecia, Finlandia y Noruega.

2. El Presidente de México en 1861 era: (a) Díaz, (b) Maximiliano, o (c) Benito Juárez.

3. Los franceses desembarcaron en 1862 en la ciudad costera Mexicana de (a) Tampico, (b) Veracruz, o (c) Puebla.

4. Lucas, dedicado a ayudar a sus compatriotas a derrotar a los franceses en Puebla el Cinco de Mayo, era (a) un general regular en el Ejército Mexicano, (b) un Indio Zacapoaztlas, o (c) un patrón Español.

5. ¿Quién iba a triunfar en la batalla del Cinco de Mayo según todo el mundo? (a) los franceses, (b) los mexicanos, o (c) los canadienses.

6. ¿Cuántos ataques hicieron los franceses antes de su derrota final el Cinco de Mayo? (a) dos, (b) tres, o (c) uno.

7. Los que apoyaban La República de México y al Presidente Benito Juárez se llamaban (a) demócratas, (b) imperialistas, o (c) republicanos.

8. Los conservadores se opusieron a Benito Juárez al principio. Ellos querían como Emperador y Empeatriz de México, a Maximiliano y su esposa Carlota quienes eran de (a) Inglaterra, (b) Austria, o (c) Grecia.

9. Después que salieron las tropas franceses y Benito Juárez regresó a México, Maximiliano (a) regresó a Europa, (b) se retiró a Querétaro, o (c) escapó a los Estados Unidos.

10. "Entre dos individuos como entre naciones, el respeto al derecho ajeno es la paz," dijo (a) Juárez, (b) Carlota, o (c) Napoleón.

RESPUESTAS CORRECTAS:
1. (a); **2.** (c); **3.** (b); **4.** (b); **5.** (a); **6.** (b); **7.** (c); **8.** (b); **9.** (b); **10.** (a).

Cinco de Mayo Pre/Post Quiz

1. Napoleon III claimed that he was sending troops to Mexico in order to recover debts owed to (a) France, Spain and England, (b) Russia, Germany and Italy, or (c) Sweden, Norway and Finland.

2. The President of Mexico in 1861 was (a) Díaz, (b) Maximilian, or (c) Benito Juárez.

3. The French landed in 1862 at the Mexican coastal city of (a) Tampico, (b) Veracruz, or (c) Puebla.

4. Lucas, dedicated to help his countrymen defeat the French at Puebla on Cinco de Mayo 1862, was (a) a regular general in the Mexican Army, (b) a Zacapoaztlas Indian, or (c) a Spanish landowner.

5. Who did most of the world expect to win the Cinco de Mayo battle at Puebla? (a) the French, (b) the Mexicans, or (c) the Canadians.

6. How many attacks did the French make before their final defeat on Cinco de Mayo? (a) two, (b) three, or (c) one.

7. Supporters of the Republic of Mexico, of which Benito Juárez was President, were known as (a) Democrats, (b) Imperialists, or (c) Republicans.

8. Conservatives opposed Benito Juárez in the beginning. They wanted as Emperor and Empress of Mexico, Maximilian and his wife Carlota who were from (a) England, (b) Austria, or (c) Greece.

9. After the French troops left Mexico, and Benito Juárez returned to Mexico City, Maximilian (a) returned to Europe, (b) retreated to Querétaro, or (c) escaped to the U.S.A.

10. "Between two individuals as between nations, respect for another's rights is Peace," said (a) Juárez, (b) Carlota, (c) Napoleon III.

CORRECT ANSWERS
1. (a); **2.** (c); **3.** (b); **4.** (b); **5.** (a); **6.** (b); **7.** (c); **8.** (b); **9.** (b); **10.** (a).

Vocabulary/Vocabulario

ENGLISH

conservatives—political group opposing Juárez
conquer—overcome by force
courage—bravery
court-martial—military court trial
defeat—loss
defend—guard against danger
execution—punishment by death
financial investments—money put to use
flee—leave quickly
foreign—not native, from somewhere else
indemnities—debts
intervention—happening between
invaders—intruders
rampart—wall of a fort
recover, regain—get back
regroup—group again
reign—rule
republicans—supporters of the republic
resistence—go against
restore—put back
retreat—backward movement under enemy pressure
royalty—family of the king
subdue—conquer
superiority—being better
suspended—stopped
threaten—present harm
throne—seat of emperor's power
triumph, triumphant—win, victorious
troops—soldiers
unfortunate—not good
unite—get together
valor—strength
withdraw—retreat

ESPAÑOL

adueñar—to take possession
amenazar—to threaten
conservadores—conservatives opposing Juárez
conquistar—to conquer
coraje—courage
defender—to defend
debitos, deudas—debts
derrotar—to destroy, to defeat
desafortunadamente—unfortunately
devastar—to devastate
Doctrina de Monroe—Monroe Doctrine
ejecución—execution
enfrentar—to confront
establo—stable
extranjeros—foreigners
hacer una reverencia—bow to the waist
Hapsburgo—Hapsburg
independencia—independence
intervención—intervention
invasores—invaders
inversiones monetarias—financial investments
muralla—rampart
oficial—official
realeza—royalty
reinar—to reign
rescatar—to redeem, to recover
reunir—to reunite
sojuzgar—to subdue
superioridad—superiority
temporalmente—temporarily
tronos—throne
tropas—troops
unificar—to unite
valor—valor